Table of Contents

www.TopTierDigitalBusiness.com

Chapter 1:
Overview of the 48 Hour Million Dollar Brainstorm

Section A: Introduction: Starting With a Broken Laser Pointer

Picture it...

It's September of 1995. A young 28-year-old man by the name of Pierre is sitting in his living room, putting the final coding touches on his personal website. This website includes information about the Ebola virus, although not very many people are going to remember that little fact in a few years.

What makes Pierre's site memorable is that he's created a marketplace – an auction site, which he calls Auction Web. And the first thing he sells on his site is a broken laser pointer for $14.83. This surprises Pierre so much that he calls his buyer to make sure the guy knows that the laser pointer was broken. The buyer knew – in fact he collected broken laser pointers.

Fast forward to the summer of 1996. Pierre's little auction site has cleared $10,000 in revenues and continues to grow, so Pierre hires his first employee.

By 1997, Pierre's site had grown so rapidly that he was able to secure $6.7 million in funding from a venture capital firm. And this was right around the time that Pierre Omidyar's Auction Web site was renamed to eBay.

I don't think I have to tell you the rest of the story. Because unless you're living under a rock, you're well aware that eBay is a large, profitable and extremely successful business. And it was all started by one guy brainstorming an idea in his living room.

Some people might think that eBay was just some kind of weird fluke of a company that started with a little idea and blossomed into a successful business. But if you look around, you'll see plenty of these sorts of success stories.

Think of Dell computers, which was started by a college kid in a dorm room.

Or Google, which was originally housed in the founder's garage.

Or even Starbucks coffee. That business was started by three friends who all chipped in about $1300 each. They modeled their first store after another successful coffee house. After a few bumps in the road, they developed a business model that worked – and Starbucks became a worldwide brand.

And the stories go on and on, with companies you know such as Apple, Whole Foods, Amazon, and even Coors Beer. But the best part is that for every well-known business that started small and grew big, there are probably hundreds of stories from successful individuals who're doing the same thing.

I know, those are big examples of billion-dollar companies. But think of it – if a multi-billion dollar company can get it's start from one little idea and an operation run out of a garage or living room, then surely you can come up with a million dollar idea.

And the good news is, there are plenty of people who've blazed the trail before you and proved that it could be done...

Take the example of Simon Hodgkinson and his business partner Jeremy Gislason. These two brainstormed a little idea that started off as a special offer for their existing info product and software customers. This little idea made $80,000 during its launch week. Within two years, this single idea had made over $3 million.

The point is, these success stories aren't flukes. These aren't rare sightings or myths like the Loch Ness Monster or Big Foot. These are real. And there are plenty of people who've brainstormed an idea, tested the idea rather quickly, and then went on to build a big and successful business around their idea.

Best of all... you can do this too, and I'm going to show you how.

You're going to learn the EXACT steps that people like Simon Hodgkinson and Jeremy Gislason take to quickly brainstorm, research, test and develop profitable ideas. And if you devote the next two days to working on what you discover inside this course, you could walk away with your very own million-dollar idea.

Maybe you already have an idea. If so, that's great – you'll find out how to refine it, test it and develop it into a true seven-figure idea.

Or maybe you have a whole bunch of ideas, but you don't know where to start or which one to pick. This course will help you with that too.

Or perhaps you're coming into this course with a dream of building a successful business, but you have no idea what kind of product or service you could offer to turn your dream into a reality. No problem – this course will walk you through the steps.

Point is, it doesn't matter where you're starting today... because within the next few days, you're going to have a million dollar idea.

So, how are you going to brainstorm and develop this idea? You're going to do it in three main steps, which is what you'll find out how to do inside this course.

So let me give you a quick overview of what you'll be discovering over the next 90 minutes or so...

Step 1 is brainstorming and researching your idea.

If you already have an idea, this step will help you refine your idea to make sure that you're on the right track. If you're starting from scratch, this chapter will walk you through the entire process of brainstorming a great idea quickly and easily. You'll be like the Michael Jordan of Brainstorming by the time you finish this chapter.

Step 2 is where you'll assess the market.

This is where you're going to do some quick and dirty research to find out if your idea truly does have a million dollar's worth of potential. You'll find out quick ways to get a feel for what your market wants, how to scope out the competition, and how to crunch numbers in a simple little formula that will show you what your idea is really worth.

Have you ever played poker and drew a royal flush? Remember the adrenaline rush you got? Remember how excited you were? This is the step where you'll recapture that feeling. Because the moment you realize your idea is worth a lot of money is the moment you'll feel like you've hit the jackpot.

Once you've confirmed that your idea has at least a million dollar's worth of potential, then you'll move on to the last step.

Step 3 is where you'll test your idea.

This is where you're going to release your idea out into the wild and let your customers vote with their wallets. But the good news is that you don't need to slave away for months or pour your life savings into your project. That's because you'll discover two quick and dirty ways to test your market – even if your product or service isn't ready to launch yet!

It's really a pretty simple and straightforward process. But what's exciting is that this is the same process countless other people have used to think up brilliant ideas which went on to become profitable businesses.

Now it's your turn…

One solid idea. One intense weekend. One million dollars!

Click on the next chapter and let's get started…

Chapter 2: Accelerated Brainstorming and Research

Section A: Introduction: Opening the Door

Jim Rohn said: "Ideas can be life-changing. Sometimes all you need to open the door is just one more good idea."

Guess what? There's a brilliant, life-changing idea already tucked away in your brain. If you're lucky, that brilliant idea has already revealed itself to you. And you're probably hopping around like a kid on Christmas morning, ready to turn your idea into a reality.

If that's the case with you, great! You're well ahead the vast majority of people that I talk to. All you have to do is take a look at this chapter just to double check that you're on the right track. In fact, working through this chapter might help you uncover an even better idea.

Now, if you're wringing your hands and worried because you don't have an idea yet, relax. The good news is that you will have a genius idea, and soon. All you have to do is walk through this chapter step-by-step, and together we'll uncover a life-changing business idea that's going to rock your world.

Here's what you're going to do:

- **Step 1, Recognize the Ideas All Around You** – in other words, you're going to do some good old fashioned brainstorming.

- **Step 2, Research Your Idea** – If you want to create a product or a service that's virtually guaranteed to sell like hotcakes, then you need to find out what your market is already buying… and give them something similar. That's what you'll do in this step.

- **Step 3, Review Your Research** – In this final step you'll weed through your ideas and choose the one that looks the most promising.

Three simple steps. Not only will you like look an absolute genius when you get to the end of this process, but you'll also be well on your way to developing a seven-figure business idea. So please move on to the next section so we can get started…

Section B: Tapping Your Inner Einstein

I've seen a lot of people give a few minutes of serious thinking to what kind of business ideas they could pursue. Then they throw up their hands and say, "Well, I can't think of anything."

Piffle.

Albert Einstein used to say, "It's not that I'm so smart, it's just that I stay with problems longer." In other words, he devoted more than two minutes of serious thinking to a problem. And if you want to come up with a great idea, then you need to tap into your inner Einstein.

So, at this step you need to do two things:

Number 1. Decide who your customers are going to be. In other words, to whom are you going to sell your products or services?

Number 2. Brainstorm solutions to offer these customers. In other words, what type of product or service are you going to sell to these customers?

In general, you should start by coming up with a market first. In other words, who are you going to sell things to? Golfers, business people, college students who want to lose weight, parrot owners, people who like to restore cars, javelin throwers who want to become better athletes… well, you get the idea. I could go on and on.

In order to start figuring out your market, just look around. Ask yourself these questions:

- What are my hobbies?
- What are my interests?
- What are my problems?
- What hobbies, interests and problems do my friends, family and colleagues have?
- What are other people interested in?

Let me give you a few examples:

- You just got a puppy – dog owners are a potential market.
- Your friend is learning to SCUBA dive – that's a potential market.
- Your cousin is trying to lose weight before her wedding – that's a potential market.
- You see on the news a piece about a large number of people connecting to Facebook through their mobile phones – that's a potential market.
- Your sister decides she's going to start knitting little sweaters for her hamsters – ok, not sure of the demand there, but that is a potential market. And those hamsters will probably look cute in their little sweaters.

Point is, look around and you'll discover dozens, hundreds or even thousands of potential markets, depending on how long you brainstorm or how much research you do. Just remember what Einstein said – stick with the problem for awhile and you're bound to brainstorm up a genius solution.

Once you've picked out a couple good market ideas, then your next task is to brainstorm what types of products or services you'd like to offer these prospective customers. Ask yourself these questions:

- What is the biggest problem this market faces?
- What types of solutions would I like to use?
- Where do the existing solutions fall short?
- How could existing products or services be made better?

Take some time and really think about the answers to these questions. For best results, use the included worksheets inside the accompanying workbook which you should have downloaded to help you brainstorm both markets and solutions for these markets.

However, take note that you may not come up with a product or service idea just from brainstorming alone. This is particularly true if you're not overly familiar with a particular market.

If that happens to be the case with you, no worries. That's because in the next section you'll find out how to spy on your market to figure out what they want. When you've finished your brainstorming, then move on to the next section and let's dig into some fun research…

Section C: Filling Your Bucket in the Ocean

Let's imagine for a moment two guys who're each carrying empty five-gallon buckets. Their task is to fill these buckets with water.

Joe goes to the Sahara Desert and starts adding a few thimblefuls of water here and there as he finds it. Pretty slim pickings.

Meanwhile, Jack goes to the ocean, takes a few steps in... and fills his bucket instantly. Mission accomplished. Not only that, he can refill his bucket a million times if he wants to.

Kind of a silly story, right? And yet a lot of entrepreneurs seek out the Sahara Desert of customers. They struggle. They fool themselves with mirages, like thinking a lot of traffic to a website means a lot of money. Eventually their whole business collapses like a thirsty man under the hot desert sun.

So here's what I suggest: bring your business bucket to the ocean of customers. That means delivering solutions to people who're already spending vast amounts of money in the market. Find an ocean of customers and cash... and then go swimming in it!

How do you find this ocean of cash? By using the following seven methods for discovering what your market wants...

Method 1: Browse Amazon

Amazon is a huge marketplace, where people can buy and sell just about anything under the sun.

Some people tend to think that Amazon is only useful for information authors who want to sell physical books or Kindle books, but Amazon is one of the biggest marketplaces online, and thus it has a wealth of information. Amazon carries a huge variety of products across a staggering number of niches.

Indeed, people are selling everything from iPod cases to concealed toilets to inflatable dinosaurs to drinking games to hiking shoes to dog treats to baby toys to Star Wars t-shirts to lawn games to water skis to protein powder to...

Well you get the idea. If a product exists, there's a good chance it's already on Amazon. And because Amazon ranks their bestselling products and lets customers review them, you can get a lot of information on this site.

So here's what you need to do: insert a few broad keywords that are related to your target market. If you already know exactly what kinds of product you want to research, then enter in the appropriate search (like "organic pest spray" as an example). Otherwise, use a broad search, like "dog training" … or "organic gardening" … or "javelins."

So let me give you an example. If you enter a really broad search term like "organic gardening," you will find:

- Organic gardening books
- Gardening videos
- Gardening tools like trowels and hoes
- Vegetable seeds
- Soil additive
- Slug control powder
- Gardening work socks
- Hemp gardening gloves
- Tree fertilizer spikes
- Hydroponics starter kits
- Concentrated fungicide
- Gardening hats (to block the sun)
- Kelp fertilizer

And that's just the short list of the sorts of items you'll find under that broad search term.

Ideally, what you'll want to do is narrow down your search by department. That's because choosing a department allows you to sort your search according to popularity. So, for example, you might choose to narrow your search to the "garden and patio" department, which will show you all the seeds, tools, fungicides, insecticides and similar products.

You're looking for two things:

1. Bestselling products.
2. The customers' thoughts about these products.

Obviously, you're looking for bestselling products because you want to know what your market is already spending their money on. If you choose a category to search in, then Amazon lets you sort your search results according to popularity.

Ideally what you should be doing is looking for evidence that there's a buying market. And if you see several of the same types of products competing in a niche, that's a good sign that there are plenty of buyers.

Let's take a classic example – search for something like "weight loss" on Amazon, and you'll find thousands of books, diet aids, pieces of exercise equipment and more. That would be your sign that it's a huge market.

The savvy entrepreneurs go a little deeper though. That means finding a chunk of the market that you can carve off for yourself and dominate. Go back to the weight loss example – if you tried to tackle the general market, you'd be up against giants like Atkins, Weight Watchers, Slim Fast and so many more.

Those guys are Goliath the Giant. You're David. And you forgot your sling shot at home. This is one fight that's gonna end fast (and it ain't gonna be pretty).

So, what you look for is a little chunk of that market that you can absolutely dominate. In the case of the weight loss market, you might niche down to new mothers who want to lose weight.

If you were going after golfers, you might focus on teenagers. Teenagers tend to have smaller hands then adults, so these youngsters would benefit from:

- Smaller golf gloves.
- Smaller clubs.
- Strategies that show them how to put a lot of power behind their drives.

If you wanted to serve dog owners, you might focus on those who own toy dogs (or even just one type of toy dog, like Maltese dogs). These dog owners with small dogs might want:

- Small toys
- Small treats
- Small dog beds
- Small dog clothes
- Small kennels
- Small agility courses

Point is, look for these hungry little niches while you're doing your research. And then look at what types of products they're already buying… and make it a goal to give them something similar (but better).

To that end, the second thing you want to do is read the reviews on the bestselling products in the niche. Check these two things:

- What do people LIKE about a particular solution? You'll want to make sure your product offers the same valuable and desirable benefits.

- What do people DISLIKE about a particular solution? These are the factors you'll want to improve upon so that you create a product that's better than anything on the market.

You'll want to spend some quality time fishing Amazon's depths. But don't make the mistake of researching Amazon in a vacuum. Once you're done with Amazon, move on to the remaining six methods for finding out what your market wants…

Method 2: Find Out What eBayers are Buying

eBay is another place where you can buy and sell just about anything. Simply enter in your broad keywords to see what kinds of solutions people are selling in your niche market. Not only can you check out the current auctions, but you can also click on "Advanced" search and take a look at the completed auctions, too.

Here's what you're looking for: Solutions that almost always sell. If you see a lot of auctions without bidders or winners, consider it a bad sign. You want to sell products that are popular, with a big market of buyers.

Method 3: See What Types of Apps People Want

If you're thinking there's a chance that you'd like to sell software or mobile phone applications, then you'll want to find out what types of apps are selling well.

Your first stop is the Apple.com iTunes Store, especially if you're interested in selling apps for iPhones or other Apple products.

Just click on any apps category, and you'll see the most popular apps in that category. You can also read customer reviews to find out what people like or don't like about particular apps.

Your next stop is the Android apps store, which you can find at: play.google.com – just click on the "Android Apps" category.

Same thing applies here as in the Apple store. Just check out the top paid and top free lists to get an idea of what's popular.

If you didn't already discover this before, take note that Amazon.com also has an apps store. Click on the "Shop by Department" dropdown menu to choose the Android app store. Again, look for popular apps and read the reviews.

And of course you can also just run a Google search for a term like "best apps." There you'll discover blogs and other websites where various users have reviewed, rated and ranked what they consider the best apps. If you find something that looks promising, then you can do further research in the apps stores to find out if the product is indeed popular.

Method 4: Discover What People Are Asking About

Think about the last time you had a problem. Maybe you had a leak in your chimney, stretch marks on your belly or maybe you just didn't know what to serve at an upcoming dinner party. So what did you do?

You probably asked someone, right? Could have been someone online, or maybe you asked a friend. But you probably didn't bust a brain cell trying to figure it out all by yourself.

You're not alone.

When people have a problem, they often ask questions about how to solve that problem. And if you're interested in creating an information product (like a book), then you'll want to know what people keep asking about in your prospective niche.

Where can you go to find these answers? Two places:

1. Quora.com
2. JustAnswer.com

LinkedIn Answers also used to be a good place for research, but they no longer support that feature of the site. You've probably also heard a lot about Yahoo! Answers. The problem with Yahoo! is that you have to spend a lot of time weeding through the juvenile "Beavis and Butthead" type questions. It's much better to go to Quora or JustAnswer, both of which have a more professional atmosphere.

Again, all you have to do is enter in your broad niche keywords – like "dog training," as an example – and you'll find out what people want to know. Look for a pattern of the same types of questions popping up again and again over time, as that's a sign that it's a common problem.

Take note – just because someone asks about a solution doesn't mean they'll buy it. So use this research to help confirm your other findings, but never use this method by itself.

Method 5: Use Keyword Tools to Uncover Desires

Another nifty way to find out what people want is to find out what sorts of queries they're typing into search engines. You can do this by using any number of keyword tools, from free tools like the Google Keyword tool, to more sophisticated tools like MarketSamurai.com.

Once again, just enter your broad keywords into the tool, and let the tool show you what people want. Be sure to enter in multiple similar terms. For example, entering both "lose weight" and "weight loss" into separate queries will give you a better picture of the overall market.

The cool thing about using a keyword tool is that you can also look for keywords that suggest the searcher is a buyer. For example a result like, "buy poodle housetraining book" gives you a good indication of what buyers want.

Method 6: Eavesdrop on Niche Forums

Still another way to get a feel for what your market wants is by lurking on the top forums in the niche. Finding these forums is pretty easy – just run a Google query for your broad topic alongside the word "forum" or even "discussion forum."

This is really similar to your research on Quora and JustAnswer, in that you're looking for patterns. Look for the following:

- What types of questions and discussion topics keep coming up again and again?
- What types of solutions are people looking for?
- What types of solution are they already using?
- How would they improve these solutions?

Once again, let me caution that you shouldn't use this method in isolation. Instead, use it to confirm your other findings.

Method 7: Survey Your Market

The final method for finding out what your market wants is... get this... ask them!

Now, it's true that what people say they want and what they actually buy can be two different things. However, you can certainly survey your market in order to confirm your research. You can ask them about:

- What types of solutions they're seeking.
- What solutions they're already using.
- What they like about those solutions.
- What they don't like about those solutions.
- What they would like to see in a product or service.

If you don't have your own blog or other website, then you can use Instant.ly (https://www.instant.ly/) to gain access to 12 million consumers, sorted by age, gender and other demographics. This service has good social networking integration, and its most basic access is free.

Once you've completed both your brainstorming and research, then you'll want to take a few minutes to review your research. That's what you'll find out how to do in Section D... see you there in a minute!

Section D: Reviewing Your Research

Before I go any further, I want to remind you of something important...

There's a manual that accompanies this course, which includes worksheets to help you with the previous brainstorming and researching steps. Please take some time to complete the worksheets, as these tools will help you complete this process more quickly and easily.

Some people complete these steps and only have a couple viable options. But most people end up with more ideas they could pursue in a lifetime.

In the next chapter you'll find out how to assess these different ideas in order to determine which ones seem to be the most viable. However, if you're starting out with quite a few ideas, then you may want to whittle down your list a bit to save time later.

To do that, ask yourself these three questions about the ideas on your list:

1. Which ideas seem to have the most profit potential, at a glance? These are the ideas that seem to have a large, eager market and plenty of products and services being offered to the larger market.

2. Which ideas personally excite and interest you?

3. Which ideas really leap out at you as good possibilities?

While you're primarily looking at these ideas in terms of profit potential, it is helpful if you personally like the idea. I mean you're going to be joined at the hip to this idea for awhile. We might even say you're going to be married to this idea.

You wouldn't get married to someone who looked hideous and with whom you couldn't stand to be in the same room for more than five minutes, would you? Of course not. And likewise, you don't want to get married to an idea that has your stomach turning and reaching for a sick bag. So choose wisely.

Now rank your ideas from best to worst, based on your answers to those questions. When you start assessing the viability of your idea in the next module, you can start with the best idea on your list and work your way down until you find your million-dollar business idea.

Let's recap where we are in the next section, and then you can move on to the next chapter...

Section E: Quick Recap

Over the last several minutes you've learned how to:

1. Recognize Great Ideas All Around You
2. Research These Ideas
3. Review These Ideas to Create a Short List

So, whether you came to this course with a burning idea, or you didn't have a clue where to start, at this point you should now have at least one if not several viable ideas.

It's getting kind of exciting, isn't it? If you like what you've uncovered so far, then you're really going to enjoy the next module. And that's because you're going to find out if your idea really is a seven figure idea. So stretch, take a deep breath, and jump right into the next chapter...

Module 3: Verify Your Million-Dollar Idea in a Snap

Section A: Introduction: Putting Your Idea Under the Microscope

You've got an idea. And if you're anything like me, this idea feels like it's coursing through your veins. It's hopping you up with adrenaline. And I bet it's going to cause a few blissfully sleepless nights as you lay awake because your idea excites you so much.

But before you unleash this idea into the wild, you need to scrutinize it a bit more. And as author Elizabeth Peters said: "I have learned that particularly clever ideas do not always stand up under close scrutiny."

In other words, maybe it's time to slap your idea on a glass slide and put it under the microscope.

At this point, you can just imagine a bunch of MBA grads sitting at a table, wearing those silly pocket protectors, doing an old fashioned SWOT analysis. Nothing wrong with that – it works for them. But for you, speed is key. We want to develop your idea and release it into the wild as soon as possible. And that's not gonna happen if you take the time to write up a 100-page analysis.

There's no need for you to spend months analyzing and researching. Because with the internet, you have everything you need right at your fingertips – and you can do some quick and dirty analysis in just a couple hours. And that means you can develop your idea in a quick weekend. No kidding.

You see, you're not just looking for clever ideas. If you want clever, you could just look at how people get their 15 minutes of fame on YouTube. (Hint: a cat is usually involved.)

That's not exactly what you want. What you're looking for are ideas that are potentially million-dollar ideas. And in order for an idea to turn into a seven-figure sum, you need to find out if there are a group of proven customers who are willing to exchange their cash for your goods or services.

There are a variety of ways to do this rather quickly, including:

- Researching with keyword tools.
- Tapping into Google's tools.
- Using Facebook's tools.
- Checking out the competition.
- Determining the value of your prospective customer pool.

So, make use of your excitement and let's do the research – see you in the next section...

Section B: Stalk the Search Engines

Back in the last chapter, you used a keyword tool like the Google keyword tool or Market Samurai to find out what types of products and services people in your market were looking for. Now it's time to return to the keyword tool to find out how many times people in your market are searching for your specific solution.

So what you need to do is go back into your favorite keyword tool, and think about what types of queries people might put into a search engine to find your solution.

Let's take a basic example. Let's suppose you decided to create an organic spray to get rid of aphids and other garden pests. You might look at search terms such as:

- Get rid of aphids
- How to kill aphids
- How to keep aphids out of the garden
- Destroy aphids
- Organic pest control

And similar queries.

To narrow it down further, you'd look for queries that indicated the searcher was specifically looking for a spray (as opposed to a book). For example, you may find search terms such as:

- Aphid spray
- Buy aphid spray
- Buy organic insecticide

And similar queries.

What you're looking for is a large market, which would be indicated by a large monthly search volume. We'll talk about specific numbers and what to do with them in a later section in this module. But first, check out the next section to find out if your market is holding steady, trending upward or declining…

Section C: Track Traffic Trends

Imagine that you decide to visit a racetrack and bet on the ponies. You look at the race line up and spot a horse named Tipsy Toesy. Since you imbibed on a few pre-race beers and are feeling a little tipsy yourself, you figure it must be a sign. So you drop your life savings on Tipsy Toesy.

That would never happen, right? You'd never drop your life-savings on a horse – at least not without thoroughly doing your research to make sure this horse is on a winning trend.

And likewise, you shouldn't jump on your big idea until you've confirmed it's trending upward, too. That's why you'll want to take a look at Google's traffic trend tool.

Google used to offer two tools: Google Trends and Google Insights. However, these tools have now been combined under one umbrella, which is called Google Trends. You can find this tool at google.com/trends.

As the name suggests, this tool shows you how specific search queries have been trending over the past nine years. What you're looking for is an indication that search queries are stable, or that they are going up.

You can also use the "insights" part of the tool, which shows you regional interest in your search term, as well as related search terms. This is particularly useful if you intend to target a particular demographic living in a particular part of the world.

Lots of great info, right? Meet me in the next section, where you'll discover another powerful way to take a peek inside your market…

Section D: Swipe Facebook's Data

Facebook lets you have a look at some of their data in two ways:

1. First, through their advertising platform.

2. Secondly, through their graph search function.

The problem with the graph search is that it doesn't give you exact numbers. Instead, if you perform a search, it just tells you if your search created over 1000 results. This will show you if your target market is way too narrow. However, it won't show you if you have a big enough target market to support a million dollar business.

The advertising platform is more powerful, because it shows you the reach you'd have if you placed an ad on Facebook. Start by going to Facebook.com/ads. From there, you'll be able to get an estimate of the Facebook audience who's interested in your topic.

For example, if you were interested in targeting women who like cats, then your audience consists of 6.3 million members. If you wanted to target men and women who're interested in golf, you'd have an audience of 8.3 million members.

Best of all, you can drill down and more narrowly focus your target market based on location, age, gender, broad interests and/or narrowly defined interests. And that means you can get a really clear idea of just how big your target market is on Facebook.

So far, we've been looking at the market. But in order to get a clearer picture of this market, we also need to take a peek at your competitors. That's what you'll find out how to do in the next section – I'll see you there in a minute...

Section E. Spy on the Competition

OK, time to do your best James Bond spy impression. Grab a martini (shaken, not stirred), grab your spy goggles, and let's take a peek at what your competitors are doing.

What you're looking for are gaps in the market, poorly positioned products, or other competitors whom you can dominate.

Contrary to popular belief, a niche market that's barren of competitors isn't necessarily a good find. Some people think it indicates there's a market to exploit. You can almost see the dollar signs lighting up in their eyes.

But that's not always the case. Sometimes a low number of competitors may indicate that the market isn't able and willing to spend money on solutions.

In other words, don't be afraid if you see a lot of competition in a particular market. Consider it a good sign, as it tells you that the market is big enough to support a lot of products and competitors. And if you can find a gap in part of the market – meaning an underserved part of the market – or if you just position yourself well to attract a subset of the overall market, then you can carve yourself off a nice slice of the market.

So, what does a market gap look like? Here are a couple examples:

- Example #1: There are several really popular competing apps available for the iPhone, but you don't see a similar strong competitor app built for the Android. You might consider creating an app for that market segment.

- Example #2: You see information products (such as videos or home study courses) that are targeted at beginners or advanced users, but you see a gap for intermediate members of the market. You might create a product to serve those in the middle.

Those are just generic examples to get you thinking about your own niche. So let me give you a real example…

Think about the types of cell phones you see today. Most of them are absolutely loaded with features, from cameras to advanced technology to run a variety of apps, play music, get on the web, video conference and so on. And it seems like each phone that hits the market has more features than the others.

These sorts of smart phones really appeal to the younger generation. However, a company named Jitter Bug spotted a gap in the market. Namely, they noticed that there was a certain segment of cell phone users, usually older people, who weren't interested in all the bells and whistles typically found on later model cell phones and smart phones.

You see, this market just wanted to use the cell phone as a phone. They weren't interested in texting, taking photos or connecting to the web. They didn't want an app on their phone that played the guitar. They didn't want to play Angry Birds. And they'd rather cover themselves in honey and lie on a fire ant hill than have an app that farted.

Simply put, this market segment just wanted a plain ol' phone.

Jitter Bug filled that gap by creating a big-buttoned, easy-to-use phone. In the United States you can see their advertisements on TV and in magazines which appeal to older people.

Point is, Jitter Bug looked at a huge market of cell phone users, and carved off a nice niche for themselves by targeting older users and those who simply weren't interested in smart phones. That's what you call finding a gap in the market and filling it.

Now, the good news is that you can do the same thing. You'll need to spend a little time researching your market, though. Here are three quick and easy steps to take...

Step 1: Search Google

The idea here is to enter your main keywords into Google, and then take note of the first two pages of competitors. You're not looking at these competitors necessarily in terms of search engine optimization. Rather, you're looking at their business model overall. Ask yourself these questions about your prospective competitors:

- How have they positioned themselves and their products in the market?
- What segments of the market are they serving – and are there any gaps?

Step 2: Check Out Competing Products

You're not going to uncover every popular product or business on the first page or two of Google. That's why you should take a trip back to Amazon and search their marketplace for competing products.

Again, ask yourselves how these products are positioned and if there are any gaps in the market.

Step 3: Browse CrunchBase.com

CrunchBase.com gives you statistics and history one some of the bigger businesses in your market. You can:

- See what all products or services a company is selling.
- Discover the company's financial history.
- Get an idea of how much traffic the site gets.

And much more. This information will help you determine who the biggest competitors are in your market. It gives you an idea of how profitable a particular market is. And it also gives you an insight into a particular company. If you want to replicate success, then study your competitors using this tool and the steps mentioned above.

Over the last few sections you've been gathering a lot of information with regards to your competitors and the niche markets they're serving. Now in the next section we're going to pull all your research and data together to find out if you truly have a seven-figure business idea. See you in a minute…

Section F: Quick and Dirty Number Crunching

Earlier I mentioned the traditional way of starting a business, which includes tedious research and analysis, such as the SWOT analysis. And, as I mentioned, there's nothing really wrong with this sort of analysis… except that it takes too long. What we want to do is spend a few hours at the computer, crunch a few numbers, and make a quick decision about whether you have a seven-figure business idea or not.

So, set aside the idea of spending weeks analyzing the market potential. Instead, grab a calculator and let's figure it out right now.

I know, you were hoping this course wouldn't require math. The good news is that you don't have to do anything hard, like figure out when two trains will meet if one leaves

New York City with a tail wind and the other leaves Los Angeles with a hefty load of Sumo wrestlers.

No worries, nothing like that. Instead, we'll crunch numbers in three easy steps. Namely:

Step 1, you estimate your prospect pool.
Step 2, you estimate the value of this market as a whole.
Step 3, you estimate how much this market is worth to you.

Let's look at each of these steps more closely.

Step 1: Estimating the Prospect Pool

What you're going to do for this step is take some of the data that you uncovered in the preceding sections. For example, take a look at just the Facebook data and what sort of audience Facebook estimates for your market.

You can certainly look at the data from multiple sources, such as looking at the data from both Facebook and your keyword research. However, if you do this the key is to look at them separately. In other words, don't combine them. If you combine them, you won't get accurate numbers.

Here's why: if someone is on Facebook showing an interest in your topic, that same person is probably also searching Google for keywords related to that interest. Problem is, you have no idea how much overlap there is.

Let me give you an example: If you see a reach of 200,000 on people Facebook who're interested in knitting sweaters for hamsters... and your main keyword is searched 200,000 times in Google, that doesn't mean you have a prospective market of 400,000. That's because you don't know how much overlap there is between the two sets of data.

So, again, just look at one set of data at a time, such as Facebook's estimated reach.

Let's say for illustration purposes that you want to find out how many people have an interest in the topic of "small business" on Facebook. Using the advertising platform tool, Facebook suggests you'd have an audience of 1.9 million people.

Now let's carve off a smaller segment of that population. Let's suppose we want to look specifically at how many people are interested in mobile marketing. Facebook gives us an audience of 174,960. Much smaller than the overall market – so let's see if our idea is viable.

Take note of these numbers and move on to the next step.

Step 2: Estimating the Value of this Market Overall

The second thing you want to consider is about how much money the average person in your market is spending on niche-relevant products and services.

Let's go back to the example of those who have an interest in small business (of which mobile marketers are a smaller segment). Just consider how much the average small business owner spends each month. For the sake of simplicity, let's assume it's an online business owner with low overhead:

- Domains, hosting, autoresponder and other tools: about $750 annually
- Employees or independent contractors: about $40,000 annually
- Product development: about $25,000 annually
- Advertising: about $25,000 annually

Again, these are just made-up figures. The actual figures would vary widely depending on the industry and what the small business owner is selling.

For example, someone who's developing software and apps is likely to have a far greater product development budget than someone who is developing books. And of course someone who sells physical products would have manufacturing, stocking and shipping expenses. So, just realize these figures aren't made to represent any particular industry.

Now, with that disclaimer out of the way...

What we can see is that an average small business owner spends over $90,000 annually. That's a good sign. Whether you're looking at the overall market (which include the 1.9 million people interested in small business) or the smaller segment (those who're interested in mobile marketing), you can see this is indeed a valuable and big market.

So, what is this market worth to you? That's what you'll determine in the next step…

Step 3: Estimating How Much this Market is Worth to You

At last – now we're going to find out if you have a million-dollar idea. Depending on how big the numbers were in the last step, you probably already know whether your idea has potential. But let's get a little more specific.

What you need to do next is estimate how much you'll charge for your product or service. One good way to estimate this is by looking at what your prospective competitors are charging for similar products and services. Depending on what you plan on selling, you may see a wide range. For the purposes of this exercise, choose a price that's at the low to middle end of the price range.

Now, let's suppose you decide that you want to sell products or services to mobile marketers for $50. Your next step is to go back to the data from step 1 (your estimated audience size) and multiply this by your estimated price in order to obtain a value for how much this market is worth to you.

Since we're getting more specific, we're going to look at just the mobile marketers on Facebook, which is an audience of 174,960 people. Let's do the calculations…

174,960 people interested in mobile marketing X $50 per product = $8,748,000

Wow – this is an $8.8 million idea.

Now, there are a couple key points to keep in mind. First, you're obviously not going to get anywhere near 100% market saturation. However, you're also looking at just one set of data from one site, which doesn't give you the full picture of your prospect pool. That's why this is a quick and dirty method.

If you end up with a higher number like our example of the market being worth $8.8 million, then you can feel pretty confident that you have a seven-figure business idea even after you factor in real data regarding market saturation and your true reach.

However, if you find that your calculations show your market is worth right around the $1 million mark, then you may want to look a little deeper. That means doing further calculations to figure out what percent of the market you can actually reach, how much it will cost you to do so, and what sort of conversion rate you can expect. Then you can decide if you truly have a seven-figure business idea.

Let's recap – see you in the next section.

Section G: Quick Recap

OK, we covered a lot of ground in this chapter. To make your research a whole lot easier, I've included some tools to help walk you through this process. You'll find these tools in the course manual.

Once you've worked with those tools, then take another breather because you've done a lot of work. In this chapter you found out how to verify that you do indeed have a million dollar idea. You did this by:

- Taking a closer look at your market.

- Checking out your competitors.

- And running a quick calculation to see if there are enough people willing to spend money with you to create a seven-figure business.

At this point, you got it -- you've verified that you have a million bucks worth of potential waiting to be unleashed from this idea. But you know what? Despite crunching some numbers, right now you're still just guessing that your idea is going to grow wings and fly. You're just speculating.

But no worries. Because in the next chapter, you're going to release this idea out into the wild and let your customers vote with their wallets. So, stretch, take a deep breath, refill your beverage if you have to… and I'll see you in the next chapter in just a few moments…

Chapter 4: Test Your Million Dollar Idea This Weekend

Section A: Introduction: Scattering Dandelion Seeds

Consider this quote by P.W. Catanese:

"Once an idea is out and about, it can't be called back, silenced or erased. You can't contain it, any more than you could put the head of a dandelion back together after the wind has scattered its seeds."

You can just picture it, right? That's good. That's because your next step is to release your idea out into the wild and let the wind scatter the seeds. This is truth time, where you're going to find out if some of your seeds are going to sprout and take root.

You see, in the previous chapter you looked at your market to see if your idea was worth a million dollars. But until you actually test out your specific product idea, you simply won't know for sure if people will buy your specific product.

At this point, a lot of business owners make the mistake of investing thousands of dollars and months or even years of their time into product development. But you don't have to do that. In fact, you shouldn't do that. Because here's the mantra that I want you to have from now on...

Start small, but think big.

You don't have to risk your life savings or an incredible amount of time in order to see if your dandelion seeds will sprout. You can get up and running fast by starting small. Not only will you get some income rolling into your bank account quickly, but you'll also be able to determine really quickly whether your idea has legs.

Best of all, you're in good company when you adopt the "start small, but think big" philosophy.

Need an example? Look no further than Steve Wozniak and his friend Steve Jobs, who together started the Apple company in Wozniak's garage. These two guys built a computer and then approached a retailer about selling their personal computer. The retailer ordered 50 units. Wozniak and Jobs were broke at the time, so they had to order the computer parts on credit in order to fulfill that first order.

They started small, with just one order. But Wozniak and Jobs thought big, which is why Apple dominates the market the way it does today.

Or let's take another example of two entrepreneurs: Simon Hodgkinson and Jeremy Gislason. These two business partners brainstormed an idea one weekend that started off as a special offer for their existing customers. When they launched the idea less than two months later, they made $80,000. Within two years their brainchild – the Marketing Main Event – had generated $3 million in sales and hundreds of thousands of dollars in ancillary sales.

How did Simon and Jeremy turn a simple brainstorm into a $3 million business in less than two years? They did it by starting small and thinking big.

And now that's what I'm going to encourage you to do too, by taking small, calculated bets. In fact, you've already done the calculations in the previous module. So now it's time to test out your idea in the real world.

That's what you're going to discover how to do in the next section – I'll see you there in a few moments...

Section B: Testing Your Idea Quickly... With Real Customers

Launching a business the proper way takes time. That's because you need to draw up a marketing plan, develop your branding, and create a full-fledged product or service.

But you know what? A lot of people I talk to jump with both feet into the planning stage of launching a business. Oh yeah, they're excited. They love the planning. But the problem is, they love the planning so much that they never get out of the planning stage.

I've heard about people who've spent weeks or months designing the perfect logo to put on their website and business cards. But they never made a dime, because they never got past the stage of creating the logo.

I've even heard about people spending weeks deciding what titles to give themselves in their business – and while they were deciding whether to call themselves founders or

CEOs or Chief Bottle Washers, their competitors made money. These folks had nice titles for their nameplates and business cards, but they didn't even manage to develop a product.

My point is I don't want you to slave over the details at this point. Instead, let's test your idea and let's scatter those dandelion seeds.

Now, you have two choices:

> #1: You can choose to test the market before your product is ready to go.

> Or

> #2: You can test a "lite" or stripped down version of your product.

What you decide to do depends on what you're selling and what sort of resources you have available. Option #2 – where you test a lite version of your product – takes more time and resources, but it does tend to be a more accurate test. Option #1 is a quick and dirty way to get a pretty good estimate of the interest in your product.

Let's look at each of these more closely, starting with Option #1…

Option 1: Test the Market Before the Product is Complete

That's right, you don't even have to have anything to sell in order to test your market. However, the key to making this strategy work is that your prospects need to think that they're actually going to buy something. Getting people to click a "buy" button is a lot better measurement of interest as opposed to merely surveying people.

However, getting people to click a buy button isn't a 100% accurate measure of interest. That's because business owners who track their statistics know that not everyone who clicks the buy button actually buys the product. Still, even if 100% of those who click a buy button don't necessarily buy, it's still a quick and dirty way to get a pretty good estimate of interest in your product.

So, what you need to is:

Step 1: Create a sales letter.
Step 2: Run a quick advertising campaign.
Step 3: Track your results.

Let me explain each of these steps in a little more detail...

Step 1: Create the Sales Letter

Here you're going to create a sales letter as if the product was already complete. One bonus of creating this letter is that it really gets you thinking of what all benefits and features you'd like your product or service to offer your customers. This will help you create a better product.

Now, the key to this step is that you need to create a professional sales letter. If you don't know anything about writing good sales copy, then go to elance.com or another freelancing site and hire a professional copywriter to create the letter for you.

The reason is because you don't want your test to be skewed negatively simply because you have poor sales copy. You can have a great concept for a product, but if the sales copy doesn't do its job, then you'll get left thinking that no one wants the product.

Picture this...

Imagine if several years back if I told you I had a new whiz bang gadget that you were gonna love.

You ask me what this gadget will do for you.

I tell you that it will take photos. But I also tell you that the photos won't be as great as your current camera, nor will you be able to store as many photos as on your camera.

I bet you'd laugh in my face and walk away. And I'd deserve it, because that sure is a crappy way to try to sell a cell phone with a built in camera.

Now, hopefully if you wrote a sales letter you wouldn't do such a dismal job of selling your product. But the truth is, if you don't already know how to write good copy, it's better to hire a professional. They know how to really sell your product so that you don't end up a bad sales page that skews your results.

So, set aside the money needed to hire a copywriter so that your test is more accurate.

Everything about the letter should look like a regular sales page... this includes having a "buy" button at the bottom of the page. The difference is that when your prospects click on the buy button, they're not taken to an order form. Instead, they see a page which tells them the product isn't quite ready yet.

Now here's the fun part – this page should actually be a squeeze page. That means that your prospects will get an opportunity to join your mailing list. That way, when you actually do launch your product, you have a list of eager prospects who're already excited about buying your product or service.

Step 2: Run a Quick Advertising Campaign

Your next step is to get real prospects in front of this sales page... and quickly. This usually means you'll need to use some form of paid advertising, such as pay per click marketing.

I'll share with you now some of the best methods. Be sure to check the workbook to get the links for these various ad programs.

Using Google Adwords:This is a good all-around testing platform. However, since people don't go to the Google search engine just for commercial purposes, you may see lower conversation rates here.

Purchasing Facebook Ads: This is a good place to test if you're looking to get a sense of the "coolness factor" of your product.

Buying Amazon Ads: Because Amazon is such a big marketplace, this is a good one for testing a wide variety of physical products, digital products or even services. It works particularly well for "gotta have it now" widgets.

Using eBay's new program: This is a favorite place to advertise, simply because you're advertising within a commercial environment. In other words, a very high number of the people seeing your ads are on the site to shop.

Teting LinkedIn Ads: This seems to work particularly well for information products, such as workshops, seminars or conferences in a geo-targeted area.

Buying Reddit Ads: Here's a good place to test tech products and gadgets.

When using these sorts of per per click programs, the key is to bid on keywords that are as narrow and targeted as possible, so that you get buyers in front of your sales page (as opposed to tire kickers and freebie seekers).

Let me give you an example. Let's suppose you're selling some sort of weight loss app for the Android phone.

The cool thing about this particular example is that both Google AdWords and Facebook Ads now allow you to promote your apps directly to the relevant device owners. So, for example, if you're selling the weight-loss app to Android phone users, then only those with Android phones will see your ad on Google AdWords. And even better, you can link your ad directly to the Google Play store, so people can buy and download your app in just a couple quick clicks.

While all of this is pretty slick, you still need to make sure you target your ads using good keywords...

A keyword like "Android app" is way too broad, because you don't know what kind of app the person wants.

A keyword like "free weight loss app" isn't any good either, because that's a query from freebie seeker, not a buyer.

A good example of a keyword is something like "weight loss Android app," which specifies both weight loss and that it's for the Android. If you mention something in your ad about the app being "affordable," then you also weed out the freebie seekers.

One additional note...

You might want to make it clear in your ad that your product is a paid product. This helps you further target your promotion so that you're attracting buyers rather than freebie seekers.

Here are four example phrases which signals to prospects that you're selling something:

- Example 1: "free shipping"
- Example 2: "discounted price"
- Example 3: "best price"
- Example 4: "PayPal accepted"

Step 3: Track Your Results

Once you've set up your advertising campaign, then you need to track your results. One way to do this is by using a tool like Google Analytics. You'll count each click of the "buy" button as a potential sale. You'll get further confirmation of interest from the smaller percentage of people who choose to opt into your mailing list.

As mentioned, this isn't a 100% accurate way of gauging interest, because people can and do click the buy button without any intention of buying a product. However, a good industry-wide guideline is to estimate that about 30%-40% of people who click the "buy" button would have completed the sale.

There are other factors that influence this rate, of course. Here are three of the biggest:

- Your industry. Certain industries have higher cart-abandonment rates.

- Where the price is located. Your price should be prominently featured just above or below the buy button, or even on the button itself. If it's not, then people will click the buy button just to discover the price, which skews your results.

- The usability of your site. Bottom line here is that if your buy button or link isn't clearly labeled as a buy button, some people may click it – even though they have no intention to purchase anything.

If you keep these guidelines in mind, you can get a pretty good estimate of interest. However, if you want to use a slightly more accurate measurement, then test the market with a lite version of your product…

Option 2: Test the Market Using a "Lite" Version of Your Product

As I mentioned earlier, developing the full version of your time can not only be expensive, but labor-intensive as well. But you don't need to develop a full version of your product in order to see if you've hit on a good idea. Instead, you can just release a lite or stripped-down version.

Let me give you a couple examples...

- Example #1: You plan to develop a complex piece of software. You can create a lite version with fewer features. This lite version will take less time for the coders to complete, so you can test the product more quickly.

- Example #2: You plan to create a home study course. Before you do that, you release a short report or even a one-hour webinar to gauge interest on the topic.

Also, recall the example I offered earlier where Steve Wozniak and Steve Jobs built one computer and used it to garner orders. They didn't drive themselves into debt or spend months building dozens of computers before getting orders. Instead, they built one computer and schlepped it around town to test the market.

Remember – start small, but think big.

Now... once you put together a light version of your product, then you need to start selling it. To do that, you must take the two steps I described earlier. Namely:

Step 1, you need to create a professional sales letter.

Step 2, you need to drive traffic to your sales letter.

Again, be sure to hire a professional copywriter if you don't know how to write sales copy. You don't want a poor sales letter to negatively affect your results.

Your next step as outlined earlier is to use a quick paid advertising method to drive traffic to your sales page. This includes Google AdWords, Facebook Ads, eBay ads, Reddit Ads and LinkedIn ads.

One of the reasons you'll want to do your test as quickly as possible is because once you've confirmed interest in your product, then you'll want to develop the full product as soon as possible. That's because your competitors are likely to get wind of the product you're testing. If they see that you have a winner, they might decide to try to replicate your success by putting out a similar product.

Point is, you want to be the first to market with your fully developed product. So don't start testing your "lite" version unless you're ready to develop your full version immediately after your test. We'll talk more about getting your product developed in the next module. For now, let's wrap things up with this module in the next section – see you there…

Section C: Quick Recap

You had a choice of testing your market with just a sales letter, or by testing it with a lite version of your product. If you're not sure which one is right for you, use the worksheet in the course manual to quickly make that decision.

There are two things I want you to take away from this particular chapter:

First, take action. Sure, starting a business takes a fair amount of planning. But the more "doing" you can accomplish alongside the planning, the faster you'll launch your business idea. And the sooner you unleash your idea into the wild, the sooner you'll find out if it's gonna sink or swim.

Since you've done your research, you're taking a calculated bet when you start testing your idea in the real world. That means you stand a darn good chance of having your idea sprout and take root. What you're doing is walking a fine line – like a tightrope over the Grand Canyon.

On the one hand, you need to do some research in order to help ensure you're pursuing a good idea. But on the other hand, you can't plan yourself into inaction. You can't sit around researching, analyzing and working on trivial details to the point where your idea never sees the light of day.

Be bold. Take action.

That's the first point.

The second point I want you to remember is to start small, but think big. Just because you're taking action doesn't mean you need to complete every single step of your business launch before you unleash your idea on the world. Skip some steps in the interest of speeding your idea to the market. Once you see that the market is interested in your product, then you can go back and complete the necessary steps.

For example, you don't need your business cards before you launch. You don't need to have a fully developed website with all the bells and whistles, when all you really need is a sales page. You don't even need a fully developed product.

Just get started. Take action. And unleash your idea on the world. Soon you'll confirm that you do indeed have a great idea. Once you do that, then you can start developing your idea more fully. That's what you'll find out how to do in the next chapter.

Chapter 5: Taking Action as Soon as Possible

Section A: Introduction: Making Room for New Ideas

"If you have a good idea, use it so that you will not only accomplish something, but so that you can make room for new ones to flow into you."

That's a quote from author and philosopher Deng Ming-Dao. Yes, this quote applies to you right now. And it's true on two levels.

First off, now that you've seen that your idea is viable, you need to do something with it. It won't do anyone any good if it never leaves your head or never leaves the planning stage.

Think of it like this – you've planted the seed. But if this seed is going to sprout, you need to take action by watering it. Just like a seed, your ideas won't sprout or bear fruit if you don't nurture them.

The second way that Ming-Dao's quote is true is that once you start taking action on ideas, you suddenly get a lot more ideas. It's like fear melts away, and gates open so that new ideas can flow freely to you.

Maybe you started this course with one good idea. Maybe you didn't even have that much when you started the first chapter. But once you start taking action, you'll have an abundance of ideas flowing to you at all hours of the night and day. Just you wait and see.

But let's not rush ahead. For right now, you need to focus on developing your business idea. And that includes doing three things:

Number 1, you need to start building a mailing list. That way, once the product is ready, you have a list of warm leads to whom you can sell your new product.

Number 2, you of course need to create the product. The good news is that you don't have to do it yourself if you're unable to or if you don't want to.

Number 3, you need to start working on branding and positioning, both of which make you stand out from your competitors.

Over the next three sections we'll look at each of these development steps in a little more detail. So I'll see you in the next section in just a moment...

Section B: Capture Customer Contacts

As you learned a little earlier in this course, you don't even need to have a product ready in order to test the market. All you need is a sales letter. And as you learned before, this sales letter should direct to a squeeze page. That way you can start creating a list of prospective customers.

However, that's not the only place where you should have a subscription form on your site. You should also create an easily accessible public squeeze page where you can start collecting leads from people who might be interested in purchasing your product or service.

Imagine for a moment that you're standing in one of those glass booths about to do a "money grab." In just a few seconds a bunch of paper money is going to start floating around you in this booth, and your job is to catch as many bills as you can in the next minute or two.

Suddenly there's a rush of air and suddenly money is everywhere. You happen to notice that most of them are twenty dollar bills. But there are also a few one hundred dollar bills floating around.

So tell me, what do you do? Do you wait for the $100 bills to float by... or do you grab everything that comes your way?

If you're smart, you'll grab everything that comes your way. And that means you'll end up with a nice wad that includes both twenties and hundreds.

The same applies here. Your customers are your one hundred dollar bills. But your prospects – people who may or may not buy – are our twenty dollar bills. Your prospects are more numerous than your customers. And you want to grab as many as you can, which is why you need to start capturing their contact info ASAP.

One good way to do this is to offer something valuable for free to your prospects. This freebie should be directly related to the product or service that you intend to sell. That way, when your product or service is ready to launch, you have a list of warm leads that you can sell to.

So let me give you a couple examples of freebies you can use to build your mailing list...

Example #1: Let's suppose you intend to sell a weight loss supplement or vitamin. You can entice people to join your mailing list by offering a fat-loss free report, which offers guidelines for helping people lose weight. Your report would plant the seed regarding how the right weight-loss supplements can help people lose the weight more quickly.

Example #2: You intend to sell a test-taking preparation app, which helps prospective graduate students prepare to take the GRE (Graduate Record Exam). To get people on your list, you can offer a free report which tells students what all they need to do in order to get into graduate school. Your free report would include an overview of the GRE test with sample questions.

Get the idea? You want to offer something valuable and desirable for free, something which is directly related to what you'll be selling.

However, do take note that you're walking a fine line whenever you start giving away valuable products for free. On the one hand, you DO want to give something valuable away. You want to use this freebie to build a relationship with your prospects and to show them that you really can solve their problems.

On the other hand, you don't want to devalue your products or services. You see, the problem with offering a freebie is that some people associate "freebie" with "no value." And so they'll associate your products or services as having no value or a low value.

So what's the solution here?

One good way to approach your freebie is by offering something that solves PART of your prospect's problem. That way, they get a taste of the kinds of solutions you can deliver. Your partial solution gets them excited about purchasing your full solution. And you don't devalue your product or service, since you're only giving a portion of it away.

So let's talk about what you need to implement this strategy:

1. The first thing you need is a squeeze page. This is a page which includes a sales letter to persuade people to join your mailing list, as well as the actual subscription form. You can build this page quickly and easily using SqueezeNinja.com – no coding experience necessary.

2. The second thing you need is a strong reason for people to join your list. This is the freebie I was talking about earlier. You might offer a free report, software, app, tool, resource, webinar, audio recording, video, multi-part ecourse, or just about anything else that's easy for you to deliver to your subscribers.

3. The third piece you need is a mailing list manager. There are self-hosted solutions available. However, you may want to use a trusted third-party email service provider, such as GetResponse.com, Aweber.com, iContact.com or any other reputable service.

Take note that I've included a checklist in the course manual to help you implement this strategy. This checklist will save you a lot of time as you work through this process, so be sure to print off a copy of it before you start building your mailing list.

For now, let me give you an overview of the process...

What you'll do is create your freebie, create your squeeze page which promotes this freebie, and then advertise the link to your squeeze page. In other words, you need to drive traffic to this page and get as many prospective customers in front of your squeeze page as possible.

Now, let me ask you something...

Imagine your best friend recommends that you go see a movie that just came out. You trust this friend's recommendation. So what do you do? Chances are, you're going to go see the movie.

Now what if a complete stranger grabbed your arm in the street and started going on and on about this movie? First thing you'd say is "back off, bro." Then you'd get the heck out of there. And you'd probably not think twice about whether you should go see the movie that the crazy old man was ranting and raving about.

Likewise, the key to making this entire email strategy work is that you need to build a relationship with your subscribers. In other words, you can't just get these folks on your list and then leave them hanging until your product is ready to launch. If you do that, they'll forget about you. The list will grow cold. You'll be like a creepy man on the street – they won't take you seriously.

Fortunately, building a relationship with your subscribers is easy. All you need to do is upload emails into your autoresponder, and set them to go out at pre-determined intervals, such as once per week.

Experts say it takes about seven to twelve "touches" in order for prospects to start to get to know you. So loading up seven to twelve emails into your autoresponder is a good place to start. You can have the first three or four messages go out every few days at first, and then settle into a once per week mailing.

Now the next question: what should you be sending in these emails? Whatever you send, the key is that the content or promotions should be directly related to your upcoming product or service. Let me give you examples of the types of content you can send:

- An email that lists one or more niche-relevant tips.
- A how to article.
- An email that whets your subscriber's appetite for your upcoming product or service.
- An email that promotes related products or services.
- An email offering another related freebie.
- An email announcing a contest.

You get the idea. The point is to offer valuable content so that your subscribers keep opening their emails from you. And the second point is to keep your name in front of your subscribers on a regular basis, so that these subscribers grow to know, trust and like you.

So that's one thing you'll be doing after you've tested your market. Another big piece you'll be working on is creating the actual product. That's what you'll learn about in the next section, so I'll see you in a few moments...

Section C: Producing Products, Lickety Split

You'll recall that earlier I told you it was important for you to develop your product quickly. That's because your competitors might just get wind of what you're working on. And the truth is, they might be working on something similar anyway... even if they know nothing about your project. So either way, you want to get your product to market first.

Obviously I don't know what you're developing, so I can't give you tips that are specific to your particular project. However, I can offer you these general tips and guidelines...

Tip #1: Remember that you can start small. Depending on what you're working on, you can release it in stages. In other words, you don't have to wait until it's completely done before you put it on the market.

For example, if you're creating a membership site with multiple features, you can open the site early and charge a smaller fee.

Another example: If you're creating a multi-part course, you can release chapters or single videos one at a time as you complete them.

Still another example: let's say your idea is to start offering a series of conferences across your country. You can start with one local conference and build from there.

Tip #2: You don't have to do the work yourself. Does Donald Trump personally hand-build all of his investment properties? Heck no. He hires experts to design and build them.

Or let's take the example of Sir Richard Branson, who started a record shop in the 1970s under the brand Virgin. Since then, Branson's company has grown to become the Virgin Group, which now consists of more than 400 companies in the areas of travel and entertainment.

Do you think Sir Branson is flying his own planes for Virgin Atlantic, writing all the books for Virgin Books, or mixing up the beverages for his Virgin Cola companies? Of course not. He outsources, because his time is better spent looking at the big picture.

Likewise, whether you're creating a book, a software, a physical product or even a service, you don't have to do the work yourself. You can hire professionals using sites like **elance.com**. If you're not skilled in the task, then these professionals will obviously do a better job than you. And better yet, outsourcing the task leaves you free to focus on other parts of your project.

The key here is to do your due diligence. That means you shouldn't go with the first service provider you find, nor should you shop around just based on price. Instead, look at the service provider's portfolio, ratings, reviews and history to determine if this is someone who not only puts out good work, but is also known for being professional and reliable.

Tip #3: Work faster, smarter and better. Chances are, your project is going to take more than a couple days to complete. And that means if you work smarter, faster and better, then you'll save yourself a lot of time, money and frustration.

While you're working on putting your product or service together, there's one other thing you need to take into consideration. Namely, branding. That's what you'll learn about in the next section... so I'll see you in a few moments.

Section D: Building a Bullet Proof Brand

Imagine that you have two entrepreneurs who put out a similar product. These two entrepreneurs are equal in every way. Their products are equal, they advertise in the same places, they have the same great levels of customer service.

Maybe they both enjoy initial success. But over time, one business owner's product sales continue to grow, while the other sees declining sales. What may have caused the difference?

In a word... branding.

You see, some business owners skip over the idea of branding their products or businesses. Generally, there are two reasons why people neglect branding:

> **1. The first reason people neglect branding is because they favor short-term sales over long-term gains**. Building a brand takes an investment of

time and money. A lot of business owners use their resources for direct sales in the short term. However, a good branding strategy pays off dividends in the long term.

Just think about your shopping habits or your friend's shopping habits, and you'll see it's true. If you're about to buy something like laundry detergent, with all else being equal, you'll probably buy the brand you already know and trust.

2. The second reason some people neglect branding is because they don't understand it. Many people think branding has to do with coming up with a slogan and a logo. But branding is much more than that. Branding is about creating a feeling.

For example, Rolex is built on a brand that's all about wealth, power and sophistication. People will drop $20,000 on a watch just to have this feeling.

Or look at something like baby products. Baby products are often branded based on feelings of love and security. Parents buy the brand that makes them feel like they're providing both extra love and security for their baby.

The point is, you're not creating this product as a short-term money-maker, right? You don't want to just shove a few dollars in your pocket for a couple months and move on. Instead, you want to build something that lasts. You want to make an impression on your prospects and customers. You want to give your prospects and customers a reason to buy from you.

That's what branding and positioning can do for you. So what I suggest you do first is go back and look at your top competitors. And ask yourself what kind of feeling they are trying to convey to their customers. Then think about what type of feeling you'd like to convey to your customers – that is, how do you want them to feel when they're using your products or services?

Secondly, ask yourself how your product packaging, slogan, colors, logo, copy and everything else can help to convey this feeling.

Let me give you an obvious example. If you sell baby products and you're looking to convey a feeling of love and family, then a bold gold and black color scheme is not going to help you with that goal. Instead, you'd look to softer colors, such as soft pinks, blues, yellows, greens and other pastel colors.

Again, keep in mind that branding is not just about colors and logos and slogans. It's about creating a feeling. Your colors, logos and slogans just help you create that feeling.

Now let's do a quick recap... see you in the next section...

Section E: Quick Recap

Getting an idea and testing it really gets the blood plumping and the adrenaline flowing, especially when you realize you're sitting on a seven-figure idea. Once you figure that out, though, then it's time to roll up your sleeves and get to work. And as you just learned in this module, you need to do three things:

Number 1, you need to start collecting leads. Don't make the mistake of waiting until your product is complete before you start looking for prospects. Find them now, get them on your mailing list, and start building a relationship with them. Then you'll have buyers lined up on the day you release your product.

Number 2, you need to create the product or service. You need to do it well, but you also need to get it to market quickly. That's why outsourcing is often a good choice.

Number 3, you need to start building your brand. That's because your brand is going to seep into everything you do, from the way you create your product to the way you package it to the design of your site. In fact, even the way you answer a customer service inquiry is going to be influenced by your brand, so it's a good idea to establish your brand somewhat early in the process.

We're almost done – just one chapter left. So go ahead and read it now – see you in a moment...

Chapter 6: Conclusion: Is Your Idea Stronger Than an Army?

Victor Hugo said, "There is one thing stronger than all the armies in the world, and that is an idea whose time has come."

That's where you are right now: One solid idea. One intense weekend. One million dollars!

You've thought up the idea. You've scrutinized it to make sure it has a million dollar's worth of potential, minimum. And if you haven't already done so, soon you will test your idea by unleashing it on your market.

It's an exciting time. You might be living on pure adrenaline for a few weeks. Your idea is going to take an almost obsessive hold on your mind as you start refining it, developing it, working on it.

But that's the key...

You need to take action. Your idea will just remain an idea if all you do is think about it. To help you out, I've prepared a checklist that you can use to make sure you're completing all the steps you need to take. You'll find this checklist inside the manual that accompanies this course.

As you learned in the last chapter, you do need to start taking a series of steps almost simultaneously. That includes developing and building your brand so that you can integrate it with your marketing messages, product packaging, website and more.

Resources

Download Your Million Dollar Idea Workbook & Checklist At The Following Link

http://peteharrismarketing.com/million-dollar-ideas-amazon-registration/

Other Books In This Series

Start Your Own Business Series

Book 2 – Start Your Own Business: How To Start Your Business On A Shoestring Budget

Book 3 – Start Your Own Business: Branding – Branding Your Business

Both available on Amazon.com

Pete Harris

I am a professional Digital Marketer & Home Business Coach. I have been a business owner for over 25 years and have vast experience in traditional and online business models.

My mission is to help as many people achieve their dreams of creating a lifestyle of choice through working for themselves and leveraging the digital economy.

You can find out more about myself at my personal blog – http://pete-harris.com

Also I have a dedicated website which highlights exciting home business opportunities at – http://toptierdigitalbusiness.com

If you require any further information then please contact me at – support@toptierdigitalbusiness.com

To your success

Pete Harris

Digital Marketer & Home Business Coach